A Note to Parents

DK READERS is a compelling program for beginning readers, designed in conjunction with leading literacy experts, including Dr. Linda Gambrell, Professor of Education at Clemson University. Dr. Gambrell has served as President of the National Reading Conference and the College Reading Association, and the International Reading Association.

Beautiful illustrations and superb full-color photographs combine with engaging, easy-to-read stories to offer a fresh approach to each subject in the series. Each DK READER is guaranteed to capture a child's interest while developing his or her reading skills, general knowledge, and love of reading.

The five levels of DK READERS are aimed at different reading abilities, enabling you to choose the books that are exactly right for your child:

Pre-level 1: Learning to read
Level 1: Beginning to read
Level 2: Beginning to read alone
Level 3: Reading alone
Level 4: Proficient readers

The "normal" age at which a child begins to read can be anywhere from three to eight years old. Adult participation through the lower levels is very helpful for providing encouragement, discussing storylines, and sounding out unfamiliar words.

No matter which level you select, you can be sure that you are helping your child learn to read, then read to learn!

LONDON, NEW YORK, MUNICH,
MELBOURNE, AND DELHI

Author Laura Buller
Senior Editor Cecile Landau
Senior Art Editor Ann Cannings
Senior DTP Designer David McDonald
Senior Producer Pieta Pemberton
Associate Publisher Nigel Duffield

Reading Consultant
Deborah Lock

First American Edition, 2013

Published in the United States by DK Publishing
375 Hudson Street, New York, New York 10014

001–192462–May/13

Copyright © 2013 Dorling Kindersley Limited

DK books are available at special discounts when purchased in bulk
for sales promotions, premiums, fund-raising, or educational use.
For details, contact:
DK Publishing Special Markets
375 Hudson Street
New York, New York 10014
SpecialSales@dk.com

A catalog record for this book is available
from the Library of Congress.

ISBN: 978-1-4654-0950-8

Printed and bound in China by
L. Rex Printing Co. Ltd.

The publisher would like to thank the following for their kind
permission to reproduce their photographs:
(Key: a-above; b-below/bottom; c-centre; f-far; l-left; r-right; t-top)

Alamy Images: BWAC Images 7. **Boy Scouts of America:** 1, 2, 3,
14-15, 49. **Corbis:** Uwe Anspach / DPA 34-35; Jocelyn Descoteaux /
Design Pics 38; Ed Kashi 30-31; David Madison 44-45; Stefano
Torrione / Hemis 12-13. **Dorling Kindersley:** Tim Draper / Rough
Guides 20-21, 48; David Peart / David Peart 38-39; Greg Roden /
Rough Guides 8-9. **Getty Images:** Yvette Cardozo / Stone 32-33;
E+ / Doug Berry 36-37; Glowimages 17, 19, 24-25, 26-27, 28-29;
Peter Arnold / Michael Sewell 11.

Jacket images: Front: **Boy Scouts of America.**

All other images © Dorling Kindersley
For further information see: www.dkimages.com

Discover more at
www.dk.com

Contents

DK READERS

READING
3
ALONE

Rapid Rescue

Written by Laura Buller

DK Publishing

Ready to Roll

Cory's phone pinged on his bedroom floor, its glow lighting up the dark room. Finally, the big day had arrived. Cory's fingers flew over the keys as he texted Chris.

"Ready to roll, dude. See you in 15?"

Cory got dressed in record time, grabbed his gear, and bounded down the stairs.

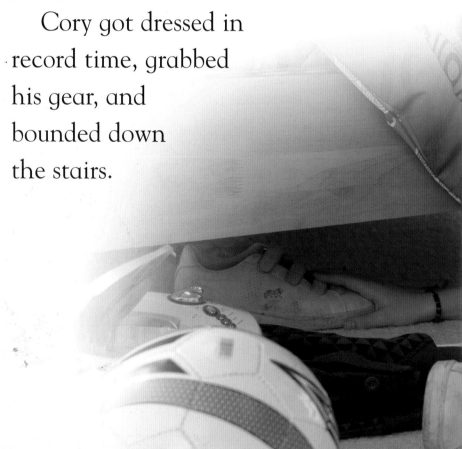

He slipped on his favorite sneakers and a hoodie, and headed out the door. Orange streaks lit the dawn sky as Cory pedaled his bike to the park. Chris and Jacob would be waiting for him there, along with the other Scouts, for the troop's first-ever whitewater rafting expedition.

A few minutes later, Cory sprinted to the waiting bus. Chris and Jacob broke away from the chattering crowd to high-five him. The three had been firm friends ever since they were Cubs.

"Nice timing, Cory," Chris said with a smile. "You're next to last."

"I can only pedal that thing, not fly on it. You OK, Jacob?" Cory said.

"More than. Today is going to be so cool. I just hope we remember all the stuff we've been learning about rafting," said Jacob. "I already had one shower this morning!"

The boys clambered on to the bus, stowed their gear and got settled. Cory crossed his fingers for luck inside his pocket, grateful for a moment that his friends could not see.

Be Prepared

The morning passed in an excited blur. Everyone was ready for an adventure! In the years since they had first taken their Scouting oaths, the boys had hiked, biked, tramped, and camped all over Wildwoods State Park. Soon the park ranger waved them through the entrance gate.

As the bus navigated the hairpin turns through the dense forest, Cory could glimpse the river through the trees. Soon they reached its placid mouth. The colorful rafts and safety gear were stacked up high.

"Let's do it!" Chris exclaimed as the troop grabbed their gear and left the bus. Cory swore he felt the hairs standing up at the back of his neck.

"Gather up, troop!"

The boys clustered around their Scoutmaster, Mr. Dale. "We're going to go through a few basics before we hit the water," he began. "First things first—your first-aid skills are critical on moving water. What could go wrong out there?"

Jacob's hand shot up. "Heatstroke? Blisters from rowing?"

"You could put your shoulder out, or scratch your arm on a branch or a rock," added another Scout.

"And there's drowning," Cory thought, without speaking.

"Troop, your CPR skills are second to none, and I know that you're ready to face whatever the river brings," continued Mr. Dale. "You've put in your time in kayaks and canoes so you're all water-worthy. To help keep you safe, we've got personal flotation

devices, helmets, throw ropes, and safety whistles. We don't hit the waves without them."

Cory raised his hand: "Mr. Dale, what is the one thing you want us to remember today?" His voice squeaked a little. Where did that come from?

The Scoutmaster thought for a moment. "Communicate. Talk to each other and use good judgment. Communicate with the river, too. Learn how to read it, how to understand it…and you'll know how to ride it. Now, are you ready?"

The troop cheered. Cory felt his stomach flip as they headed off to collect their safety gear.

He was with friends he trusted, he knew his way around the water, and he'd been excited about this trip for weeks. But now he was feeling something different…something a tiny bit like fear.

Silently Cory collected his paddles and safety gear.

A Rip-Roaring Start

"Go, go, GO!"

Cory, Chris, and Jacob pulled their raft by its ropes to the river's edge. The crystal blue water glinted in the sun. "Let's read the river," Chris said. "The water's moving south, and there aren't any worrying waves out there."

"I don't see any big rocks or downed tree branches ahead," added Cory. "This looks like where we start."

Splat! The boys hoisted the raft into the water where it landed with a noisy splash. The raft bobbed to and fro as the boys scrambled aboard, but soon they were balanced and pushing off from the bank.

They dipped their paddles into the icy river and began a steady forward stroke. Away they went!

Cory soon forgot his fears and concentrated on the river. The raft was totally at the mercy of the current, and his job was to try and keep it moving in a straight line. That was the idea, anyway!

Chris scanned the rushing river ahead, keeping a look out for danger. Jacob listened as the river's roar got louder and louder, a signal that a rougher ride was just around the bend of the river.

As they rounded the bend, the raft picked up speed. The water was churning now, white with foamy bubbles. They were starting to turn around. Cory quickly pulled the stern of the raft in line with the bow again, using a stroke called the stern draw.

He used his paddle like the rudder of a boat to even things up.

Woosh! The raft rose up in the air as they shot the first rapid.

The raft smashed back into the waters. For a moment, the boys were silent, but then they burst into relieved giggles.

"Whoa," said Jacob. "That was intense."

"And it was only the first little rapid," Cory replied. "Imagine what riding a real beast will feel like?"

"Nice work keeping us steady, Cory!" added Chris. As the friends raised their paddles to high-five with them, they took their eyes off the river for a moment. No one spotted the jagged rock they were rushing straight towards.

Rrrrippp! The sharp rock tore through the side of the raft like scissors through paper, and scraped against Jacob's bare leg. Tiny drops of blood stained the water on the floor of the raft.

"Jake! Are you OK, buddy?" shouted Cory.

"It stings a little, but I'll be fine," he answered. "Who gets patched up first, me or the raft?"

"Here, Cory, catch!" Chris unhooked the dry-storage container, grabbed the first-aid box, and pushed it across to Cory with his paddle. He kept the patch kit himself.

Cory opened the box just as they hit another patch of bubbling ripples, nearly spilling the contents overboard. He found the antiseptic wipes, handing a couple to Jacob so he could clean his wound, before covering it with a waterproof bandage. It would have been an easy task on the ground, but it was tricky to keep a steady hand while racing along the river. Meanwhile, Chris stuck the fixing patch onto the slippery side of the raft.

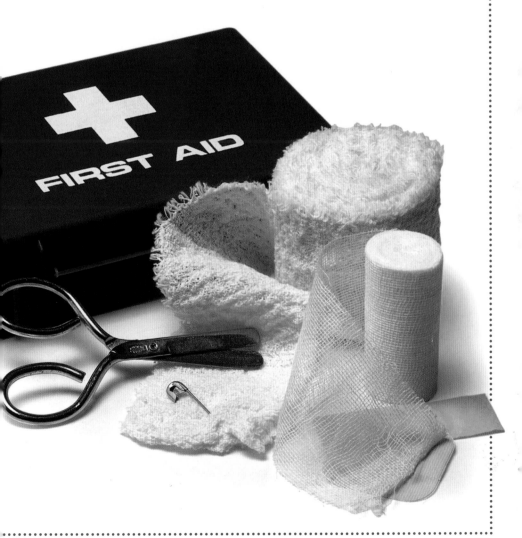

Into the Rapids

With both Jacob and the raft patched up, the Scouts continued on their course. Chris helped them navigate by calling out commands. Each time an obstacle appeared, he gave instructions so everyone knew where to put the paddles.

The boys knew from their kayaking experience that right turns called for paddling on the left, and left turns paddling on the right, but it made it much easier having Chris's instructions to guide them.

The sunlight streamed through the trees to dapple the surface of the water. The river unwound into a straighter path. "All forward!" Chris cried out.

The river flowed swiftly, but now the boys were getting the hang of negotiating the watery roller coaster. Their raft bounced along the bubbling water, twisting and turning from side to side. Sometimes the water slopped into the raft or showered the boys with a freezing-cold blast of spray, but they were making good progress. It was great fun, too.

Cory thought about how anxious he'd felt just hours ago. Now, he felt ready for more. He could hear the water's roar in the distance. It grew louder than before.

"Rapids, coming right ahead!" Chris shouted loudly above the rushing river.

The boys braced themselves for
the worst. As the raft shot through
the turbulent water, Cory felt like he
was in a giant washing machine. The
front of the raft lifted up and nearly
bent double under the force of the
pounding water. For a second all the
boys could see was the floor, then the

raft crashed down again, and everything
disappeared in a solid wall of spray.

The water knocked the paddle right
out of Jacob's slippery hands. He tried
to rescue it, but a rip current carried it
away from his grasp. All of a sudden,
the raft caught on something and the
boys lurched forwards.

They were hung up on a huge tree branch that had fallen into the river. The boys were trapped.

"Now where did that come from?" Cory said. "And how do we get unstuck from this thing?"

"I read about this once," exclaimed Chris. "We need to shift our weight around to the opposite side of the spot where we're caught."

The boys slid gently away from
the branch. The raft rocked and
wobbled dangerously from side to
side. Cory was sure one of them was
about to take an unexpected bath.

"Now, put your paddles in the water and push against the current," Chris advised.

Jacob gave him a small grin. "My paddle has gone for a swim downriver," he said.

Chris rummaged in the kit box, lifted out a spare paddle, and tossed it over to Jacob, who caught it...just.

"Come on, let's push now. Let's make like a tree, and leave!" Chris joked.

Slowly they eased their way off the branch and back into the moving water. Cory inspected the raft for damage, but it looked as if the raft was still intact.

A Sticky Situation

Chris spotted an eddy ahead and the Scouts guided the raft into the calmer part of the river for a break. They rehydrated with some bottled water, put on a fresh layer of sunscreen, and made sure Jacob's bandage was holding fast.

Chris, already soaked to the skin, slipped over the side of the raft for an impromptu swim. He was just about to pull Cory overboard when the riverbed rocks shifted suddenly with a crack. Chris's face twisted in pain. "My ankle…it's twisted."

Cory splashed into the water. "Let's get you up, dude."

Chris paled. "I…can't. I'm…stuck. My foot is trapped under this rock."

Cory assessed the situation. The water was clear enough for him to see Chris's sneaker wedged under a large stone. It looked way too heavy to move, and he didn't want to risk hurting Chris's ankle even more.

"Fulcrum!" Jacob exclaimed suddenly.

Cory closed his eyes and tried to remember last week's science project. Suddenly, he got it! By balancing some sort of pole on a pivot, he could lift an object…say, a rock…with much greater force. The machine, called a fulcrum, had been around since ancient times.

He spotted a smaller rock and moved it into place. What to use for a pole? Jacob seemed to read his mind, handing him a paddle. Would Cory make it work?

He eased the wedge of the paddle under the rock, being careful of Chris's foot. Balancing the arm of the paddle on the second rock, he began pushing down on its handle. Incredibly, the heavy rock started to lift away.

"Yes!" hissed Jacob. "I knew there had to be a good reason to pay attention in science class."

Chris tried to smile but winced in pain as he pulled his foot free. Cory gave him his shoulder in support as they made their way to the raft. He helped him inside as gently as he could.

Thankfully the first-aid box contained a bandage. Jacob and Cory wrapped up Chris's ankle. Their friend was clearly in pain, and they needed to get him some help soon. The problem was, they were right in the middle of a river.

Cory made Chris as comfortable as possible, propping his foot on a spare flotation jacket so it did not get

banged around. Although they were down to just two rowers now, Cory was determined to get home, and get some help.

"Jacob, for the second time today, let's do it," he said. They set off.

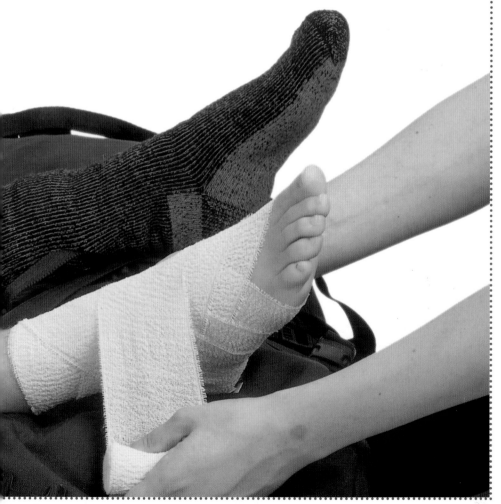

The Final Challenge

Jacob and Cory paddled as fast as they could. They were concentrating so hard, they didn't notice the sound of the water getting louder, almost deafeningly so.

"Waterfall," Chris whispered.

"What?" said Jacob. "Did you say…"

"WATERFALL!" Cory shouted. The river foamed white, pulling the raft along by strong and scary currents. In an instant they were at the fall's edge. In another, they were going over!

The boys crouched down low and clung tightly to the raft's ropes as the craft shot off the falls. Cory's mind was racing: what if there were rocks below? What if they couldn't hold on? What about Chris and Jacob? Time seemed to stop, although that was hardly possible.

SPLASH! Their raft hit the water so hard it was submerged. But then, incredibly, it started to rise, breaking the river's surface.

Cory looked over at his friends. They were shaking, and soaked through, but they were OK. Everything was going to be OK.

Mr. Dale pulled the ice pack off Chris's swollen ankle and prepared a new bandage. "I know it hurts, Chris, but the good news is, your ankle isn't broken," he reassured him. "You certainly picked the right rafting crew."

Jacob and Cory smiled as they stowed the gear for the ride home. This morning everyone had been chattering and excited. This afternoon was quiet. The river had tested the best of them, and they'd come through it a little wetter, but a little wiser, too. The bus doors slammed shut and Cory took one more look at the sun setting on the river. We did it, he thought to himself. We were ready.

Glossary

Antiseptic
A substance that kills germs, preventing infection

Canoe
A light, narrow boat, moved by paddles

Current
Flow of water that is often strong and fast

Eddy
A small whirlpool

Floatation device
A device to keep you afloat in water, such as a life jacket

Fulcrum
Support on which a lever rests and pivots when lifting something

Hairpin turn
A sharp bend in the road

Heatstroke
A high fever, caused by exposure to the sun

Hike
To take a long walk in the countryside

Kayak
Enclosed canoe with openings for the paddlers to sit in

Navigate
To steer or direct a boat, or other craft

Paddle
Pole with a broad, flat end, used to propel a canoe through water

Raft
A flat, open structure that floats, such an inflatable rubber boat

Rapids
A fast moving part of a river or stream

Rehydrate
To drink lots of water, quenching your thirst, after doing something strenuous

Roller coaster
A ride or trip that involves lots of dips and sharp turns

Rudder
A flat, hinged piece of wood or metal at the back of a boat, used for steering

Stern draw
A stroke used when paddling a canoe or raft to help keep it on course

Throw rope
A rope, loosely wound up in a bag, so it can be thrown to a swimmer in distress

Turbulent
Fast moving, swirling

Waterproof
Repels or keeps out water

Whitewater
Foaming, fast-moving part of a river